contents

Preface   Kevin Schafer   **14**

Introduction :
Tropical America   **18**

The Forest Floor :1
32

2: The Understory
68

The Canopy :3
108

Resources   **140**

Index   **142**

I first traveled to the tropical rain forest in the early 1980s on a trip with my father, a devoted birder and jungle-phile, to Guatemala and Belize. For me, it was not a case of love at first sight. I found myself gasping at the heat and humidity, annoyed that the emblematic animals of the rain forest—the monkeys, toucans, and parrots—were invariably hidden and impossible to see. Yet, despite this inauspicious introduction, I would be drawn back to the tropics dozens of times in the years that followed.

Rain forest photography, which was to become my specialty, has always been something of an ambivalent calling. From the beginning, I found the rain forest to be an enchanting, fascinating, and utterly maddening environment in which to work. Simply said, the tropical forest is a terrible place for photography. The heat and humidity can be stultifying and relentless, and often causes equipment—and photographers—to malfunction and fail. Hordes of biting ants, bloodthirsty mosquitoes, unspeakable parasites; I've had them all.

However, the rain forest's greatest challenge is simply that it is dark. Beneath the dense forest canopy is a world of shadows, an environment inherently hostile to light-sensitive film. There are no glorious sunsets inside a rain forest, no golden glow of dawn—things that gladden the heart of every photographer. In addition, most of the animal activity, particularly among mammals, takes place at night.

Mexico

HAVANA

Cuba

MERIDA

Haiti

Dominican Republic

TROPIC OF CANCER

Belize

Honduras

Puerto Rico

Jamaica

Nicaragua

Dominica

El Salvador

Venezuela

Panama

Tobago

Guatemala

CARACAS

Guyana

Costa Rica

Orinoco

Surinam

French Guiana

Colombia

BOGOTA

R.

MONTANE RAINFOREST

LOWLAND RAINFOREST

EQUATOR

R. Negro

MANAUS

BELEM

Ecuador

QUITO

R.

Napo

A m a z o n

R.

LOWLAND RAINFOREST

B
r
a
z
i
l

MONTANE

Peru

LIMA

RAINFOREST

LA PAZ

BRASILIA

Bolivia

TROPIC OF CAPRICORN

So why, with this litany of horrors, do I bother? Because I have always been fascinated by the intricacies of the natural world and the astonishing miracles of evolution, and for these, there is no greater stage than a tropical forest. Bugs that defy description, birds of the most brilliant colors, mammals of such power and grace—these are the reasons I keep going back.

I also managed to stumble into the rain forest at about the time when its wholesale destruction was beginning to attract worldwide attention. My early pictures of rain forest animals laid the groundwork for my professional career, and I am proud that my pictures have played a part in efforts to educate people about the value of the rain forest and the creatures it contains.

Meanwhile, the rain forest presents an inescapable conundrum: although animal life can often be abundant, it is almost invariably difficult to see. For that reason, while simply seeing an animal is a significant accomplishment, getting a decent picture of one presents an enormous challenge. Some animals I have never managed to photograph successfully in the wild, although I may have glimpsed them several times over the years.

Most notable among these are the wild cats. Although I have seen jaguars and ocelots in the wild, I have never taken a publishable picture of either one. The photos of the cats in this book, therefore, are of captive or habituated animals, because I felt that their presence was essential. Also captive is the extremely rare spectacled bear. Otherwise, all the pictures in this volume are of wild creatures, taken in their natural habitat. I have not included any pictures that have been manipulated by computer, for although such pictures may have their place, they don't belong in a book of this kind.

Finally, a word on behalf of the animals themselves. Some of those pictured here are extremely rare, and in many cases, critically endangered. Some, like the giant river otter, the jaguar, and the woolly spider monkey, will almost certainly go extinct within our lifetime if their habitat is not strenuously protected. It would be tragic if photographs like these were all that remained of them in the new millennium, yet this possibility is all too real. I'd like to ask everyone who reads this book, or looks at the faces it contains, to find a way to contribute toward protecting the forests and the creatures within them.

—Kevin Schafer

introduction :
tropical america

Girdling the globe at 23 degrees 5 minutes north of the equator lies an imaginary line known as the tropic of Cancer. Equidistant below the equator lies Cancer's counterpart, the tropic of Capricorn. These two latitudinal lines, 2,800 miles apart, define the Torrid Zone—the tropical region of consistently high temperatures that seldom vary more than five degrees from high to low.

Here, in the tropics, the sun approaches near verticality, delivering its warming rays directly to the earth below. Within this wide band of warmth and humidity grow the rain forest habitats that characterize much of Central and South America.

Miles-high mountains and rolling tree-clad hills thrust upward here to meet the sun's rays. Rushing hillside streams and broad slow rivers wind irresistibly to thicketed shores of the Atlantic and Pacific Oceans. In places, dense rain forests of broad-leaved evergreen trees still spread to the horizons despite a century of relentless deforestation.

Diverse in topography, in climate, and in appearance, the rain forest is a phenomenon of major importance to the world we live in. So productive are the world's rain forests that on just 6 percent of the earth's surface, they harbor more than 50 percent of the world's plant and animal species. Of these, the rain forests of Latin America are arguably the largest and, in the fantastic diversity of wildlife they host, the most important in our global ecology.

Within the Torrid Zone, winter and summer are inappropriate concepts. More practical designations are the dry season and wet season, the first distinguished from the second only by volume of rainfall.

By definition, a rain forest receives at least eighty inches of precipitation throughout the year. In many rain forests, rainfall far exceeds the eighty-inch minimum. For example, at one spot in Colombia's Choco Forest lowlands, an astonishing 463.5 inches of rain once fell in a single year.

Normally, wet season rainfall in the watershed of the vast river-bottom dish known as the Amazon Basin causes the Amazon River to rise fifty feet at Manaus, where the Rio Solimoes and the Rio Negro come together. Much of the vegetation in the basin's 800 million acres disappears beneath the flood, leaving only hills, ridges, and river levees above water.

Not surprisingly, the Amazon River attracts controversy among countries competing for a spot in the record books. Without question, the Amazon drains the greatest volume of water. It carries two-fifths of the world's fresh water to the Atlantic Ocean. New data suggest it is the longest river, as well. Recent observations made via satellite establish the "most distant mouth" of the Amazon's estuary at Pará. This additional 195 miles bring the river's total length to 4,195 miles, compared to a length of 4,150 for the Nile.

Scarlet Macaw
Ara macao

The best known members of the parrot family, scarlet macaws range from Mexico down into Bolivia. Up to three feet long and brilliantly colored, they are the only macaw to be found on both the Atlantic and Pacific coasts. In flocks of 10 to 50 individuals, macaws range widely over many miles of lowland rain forest in search of seeds and nuts, using their powerful beaks to cut through hard shells.

Blessed with a constant supply of rain and sunshine, broadleaf woodlands flourish. Rain forests spread across the Torrid Zones of Africa, Asia, Australia, and South and Central America, and tropical islands such as the Philippines, New Guinea, Cuba, and Puerto Rico.

The Neotropics (Latin America plus the islands of the Caribbean Sea) account for roughly half of the world's rain forests. Of these 2.2 billion acres, 88 percent lie within South America, 70 percent in Brazil, with the remaining forest acreage divided among Central American nations, the tropical states of Mexico, and the Caribbean islands. Altogether, tropical American rain forests extend over thirty-two countries, with elevations ranging from seashores to the flanks of cordilleras rising more than two miles above sea level.

Of the original rain forest of tropical America, about 1.5 billion acres remain more or less intact. Of the rest, about 52 percent has been cleared by small farmers for agriculture, 11 percent for cattle pasture, and most of the remainder for plantation crops such as coffee and bananas.

Rain forests have been home to indigenous peoples for 30,000 years, with impressive societies beginning to develop about 12,000 years ago. When Columbus arrived in 1492, there were, by one estimate, 30 million Indians throughout the American tropics. Within a century, their numbers had declined to some 2 million. Even today, rain forest lands remain thinly populated. The Amazon Basin, for example, with an area as large as the United States, counts a population of just 19 million people. Some fifty Indian tribes still live in parts of the basin so remote that they have never been exposed to modern technology. However, their isolation is threatened by ongoing exploration for oil and gold, logging, and colonization, all activities potentially injurious to the pristine nature of rain forests.

Ecologists speak of three kinds of rain forests. Largest and best known are the lowland rain forests, such as those of the Amazon and Orinoco River Basins. Smaller are the montane rain forests, which grow on foothills and mountainsides. The latter are found mostly in Central

Amazon River in the Dry Season
Brazil

Whether in the form of rain, mist, fog, cloud, dew, or humidity, fresh water is the quintessential element of rain forests throughout the tropics. By definition, a rain forest must receive at least 80 inches of moisture applied regularly throughout the year. In lowland rain forests, rain storms occur often, even in the so-called dry season. In montane rain forests, fogs and mists of oceanic origin roll in to soak the hills and their vegetation. Cloud forests, such as those of the Peruvian Andes, are robed in cloud banks pierced only occasionally by the sun, and water droplets form on every leaf and flower.

Angel Falls

Venezuela

In 1935, North American aviator Jimmy Angel flew over Auyan-tepui in Venezuela and spotted the highest waterfall on earth. In two steps, the water drops 3,300 feet to form the Churun River at the base of this mesalike remnant of the ancient Guianan Shield. A *tepui,* or "mountain" in the Penon tongue, is a tableland soaked by up to 150 inches of rain a year. Ten thousand plant species have been found on tepuis, half of them endemic.

America and southern Brazil and on both flanks of the Andes Mountains. The third and smallest group, occupying the intertidal zone along coastal littorals, are the mangrove forests. Though small in area, they rank among the world's top producers of biomass, the total weight of everything living in an ecosystem.

Life in the rain forest is lived within layers, from the ground level on the forest floor, through the understory in the middle, and up to the topmost canopy. Each segment constitutes first a neighborhood where highly specialized creatures live, feed, and breed, and second, a hunting ground for equally specialized predators. The divisions are not absolute. Animals may move up or down, foraging in the canopy today, the understory tomorrow. Some may feed in the understory and descend to the forest floor to drink.

In like manner, the animal and plant life characterizing each layer change somewhat with locale and altitude, as the land rises from lowlands into foothills and up to the cloud forests that drape the flanks of the towering cordilleras.

Of the 250,000 species of plants that have so far been identified and named, just 1 percent have been tested for medicines useful in the fight against disease. From this small subset have come 25 percent of all prescription drugs and medicines.

Tropical forests have yielded chemicals to treat or cure diabetes, malaria, heart conditions, skin disease, inflammation, rheumatism, muscle tension, surgical complications, arthritis, glaucoma, and hundreds of other maladies. Stimulants, tranquilizers, and contraceptives come from rain forest plants.

Rain forests are the original source for fruits such as bananas, vegetables such as peppers and okra, nuts such as cashews and Brazils, beverages such as coffee, tea, and cola, vegetable oils such as palm and coconut, flavorings such as vanilla, cocoa, sugar, and spices, and food items such as beans, corn, and potatoes.

Red-rumped Cacique

Cacicus haemorrhous

Fruit-eating forest dwellers that prefer the edges of open spaces, red-rumped caciques have learned to keep their eggs safe by hiding them within pendulous nests of grass and straw that dangle from the branches of trees. Because botflies kill cacique chicks by laying eggs in their bodies, cacique parents have also learned to protect their young by building their nests close to colonies of bees and wasps, the vigorous enemies of botflies. The generic name may have been adapted from the Spanish word, *cacique,* for the oriole, or from the Indian word, *cazique,* for chieftain.

From tropical forests come beautiful and valuable woods such as mahogany, teak, ebony, rosewood, balsa, and sandalwood. Many of the most prized flowers and decorative plants originated in rain forests, including the showiest of the orchids, bromeliads, and palms. Forest fibers supply material for rugs, mattresses, ropes, kapok, and cloth. Forest oils, gums, and resins show up in rubber products, fuels, paints, varnishes, cosmetics, soaps, shampoos, perfumes, disinfectants, and detergents.

Along with its flora, the rain forest shelters fauna of a variety and in a number unmatched elsewhere on earth. One estimate—admittedly, an educated guess—places the probable number of species at 30 million. Another estimate suggests 10 million. Either way, the number is staggering. No less staggering is the thought that this reservoir of potential knowledge could be lost by inattention or indifference.

Large-billed Tern

Phaetusa simplex

Where rain forest rivers enter the sea, large-billed terns feed by coursing back and forth in search of a surfacing minnow and plunging or swooping to seize it. During the tropical dry season, falling water levels expose broad sand banks that large-billed terns use as nesting sites. This tern's name, Phaetusa, originated in Greek mythology as that of a daughter of Phoebus (the Sun) and Clymene (a sea nymph). Turned into a poplar tree, Phaetusa's tears solidified into amber, the color of the large-billed tern's beak.

Passionflower

Margay
Leopardus wiedii

At home in the understories and canopies of all tropical American rain forests, the pretty little margay easily outclimbs such tree dwellers as monkeys and squirrels. About the size of house cats, margays have flexible ankles that enable them to descend a tree trunk head first or to hang from the underside of a branch by means of claws in their soft, wide paws. Like their bigger and better known relations, margays range the forests of the night, but usually well above ground. They will eat fruit and insects, but prefer such canopy creatures as birds, opossums, squirrels, monkeys, sloths, and porcupines.

Royal Flycatcher
Onychorhynchus coronatus

Most of the time, the royal flycatcher male is just another "little brown bird," scarcely discernible from dozens of other tropical flycatchers that thrive on rain forest insects. But when he is courting a female or threatening another male, the royal flycatcher raises his spectacular crest of orange and blue. To protect their young, a royal flycatcher pair will construct a long slender nest out of straw, grass, and vines that hangs down three to four feet from a tree branch. A pocket in the center contains the eggs where they are safe from marauding vine snakes.

Waterfall
Brazil

Canaima Lagoon
Venezuela

La Laguna de Canaima in Venezuela was
once the site of a Penon Indian village, but
its beauty and proximity to Angel Falls has
now made the lagoon a tourist destination. It
is situated in the heart of the huge Canaima
National Park, established in 1962 as the
largest park on the continent, embracing
11,600 square miles of the Guiana Highlands.
The lagoon formed by the Carrao River fea-
tures white sand beaches and transparent
black water stained by tannin. Wildlife and
plant populations are exceptionally rich.

1 : the forest floor

Forest Floor

Costa Rica

Rio Napo

Ecuador

One of the Amazon River's major tributaries, the Rio Napo drains the eastern slopes of the Ecuadorian Andes, gathers volume in passing through the rain forests of northern Peru, joins the Rio Amazonas, and surges into northwestern Brazil to create the world's largest and longest river. In this ecosystem where freezing is unknown, moisture is plentiful, and sunshine constant, vegetation thrives as nowhere else on earth. Competition among flora for nutrients, light, and water coupled with the need to survive the onslaught of plant-eating fauna has led to an amazing diversity in plant communities. Thus the rain forests of tropical America sustain around 100,000 vascular plant species, or up to 40 percent of the world's vascular plants.

The forest begins with its floor, the foundation for all that grows and lives above. In the lowlands, the forest floor differs dramatically from those typical of the montane or cloud forest habitats.

About ten hours by boat northeast of Manaus in the Brazilian state of Amazonas, the River of the Calabash Trees meanders slowly down to the Black River and, eventually, to the Amazon itself. The vegetation crowding the river's banks in this classic lowland rain forest rears tall and dense, a glittering green wall flourishing in the sun. Here, with ample water and sunlight, plant life braids itself into a forbidding and impenetrable tangle.

But within a few yards from the water's edge, the bush thins and the forest floor becomes more open. Far overhead, a leafy umbrella cuts off the sun. Of the blast furnace of nurturing light that bathes the upper canopy, just a fraction penetrates to the earth below. Here, in perpetual gloom, only the hardiest of seedlings survive in the sunless spaces. Plants that have learned to live with a minimum of light hold sway.

A layer of humus covers the ground. A soft and soggy conduit for water and nutrients, it serves as a buffet for thousands of species of invertebrate crawlers and hoppers. Through the motionless and humid air, leaves helicopter ceaselessly from the canopy overhead, adding to the supply.

To hold themselves erect in a layer of topsoil just a couple of inches thick, the forest

giants spread out their root systems like great feet. Some, like the group known as paddle trees, erect fantastic flying buttresses to shore up their trunks and hold aloft their high-flying green spinnakers to soak up the sun. Others, such as Brazil trees, manage with a thick web of surface roots spread out horizontally over a wide area. Certain palm trees ignore the soil entirely. Their roots, affixed to the trunks of nearby trees, grow upward instead of down and extract nutrients from water flowing down the host tree trunk. Mangroves hold their trunks aloft with stiltlike roots that serve as props.

Though deprived of direct sunlight, life flourishes on the leaf-

littered floor of these dim damp basement rooms.

Here, the fearless fer-de-lance lies in wait with poisonous fangs for a careless frog, but on hearing an odd rustling sound like sand sprinkled onto dry paper, slithers away in alarm. Its senses have picked up the patter of a million clawed feet scrambling over dead leaves. From deep in the forest flows a regiment of army ants in a red stream a foot wide. They are searching for prey in the form of other leaf-litter creatures to kill and eat. The column seems to vibrate as the rusty red insects march lock-step, each in touch with the next link in the chain.

Army ants are among the most feared of the rain forest's organisms. Even jaguars go out of their way to avoid the painful bites of these suicidal soldiers, who will attack any living thing perceived as a threat and die by the thousands in defense of the colony.

Arriving in an area identified by their scouts as having a plentiful food supply, the invading column fans out across a thirty-yard-wide front and begins its drive for game. Beetles and caterpillars try to hide; snails and turtles go inside and shut the door. Frogs and grasshoppers leap for safety. Snakes, lizards, and mice try to outrun the horde. Some get away, but many do not. In their frantic flight, they become prey to a hovering airforce of birds that follows the ant scavengers to pick off the refugees as they abandon caution.

Just ahead of the advancing ants, other opportunistic feeders await. The coati, for example, with a tail like a raccoon's, a head like an opossum's, and an omnivorous appetite, hustles along the forest floor to nab insects, snakes, and lizards rushing to escape the ants. The catlike bush dog, too, prowls ahead of the ants in search of the more edible frogs among the 1,600 species native to the tropical American rain forest.

Having cleaned out an area, the army ant colony builds a temporary camp in the soil to store its game, lay eggs, and hatch out new platoons to carry on the next campaign. From the moist lowlands through the dry foothills into the high cloud forests, army ants succeed as a cohesive society by virtue of a collective intelligence. The solitary ant is helpless, but a group becomes a formidable organism.

With sluggish rivers and countless lakes where aquatic vegetation flourishes, lowland rain forests shelter water-loving animals, such as the capybara, giant river otter, and tapir, along with water dwellers, such as the spectacled caiman, the anaconda, and the Amazon turtle. Strangers to the montane rain forests and high-country cloud forests, these aquatic and semiaquatic creatures flourish in a lowland habitat that expands during the rainy season to drown millions of acres of forest and make fresh food supplies available.

On the downside, when the dry season reduces the water supply, rivers and lakes shrink into their narrow channels. Aquatic life crowds into a diminishing habitat, making life harder for some, easier for others.

The drowned forest reappears. Monkeys and birds spread gleefully

Army Ants
Eciton burchelli

Of all the fauna in the rain forest, the creatures most feared by other living things may be the army ants when they sally forth on a raid. They attack at dawn; up to a million individuals stream forth in a foot-wide column until encountering food in the form of other insects, grubs, larvae, caterpillars, and even small lizards. Once a productive area is found, the army fans out to advance over a wide front, capturing and killing whatever is unable to escape. Even jaguars make themselves scarce when the army ants are on the move.

Capybara
Hydrochaeris hydrochaeris

He's the world's largest rodent, present throughout the rain forests of South and Central America. No Mickey Mouse, the capybara can grow to well over 100 pounds in weight. Daytime feeders, capybara herds of up to fifty in number inhabit flooded grasslands and marshy areas near rivers and lakes where they feed on water plants and browse on grasses. True to its scientific name, which translates as "water joy," the capybara is semiaquatic. Officially sanctioned as acceptable food on Fridays in Catholic Venezuela, capybara meat is sold in markets as honorary "fish."

over a greatly expanded range to feed on new growth. Capybara and tapir families forage the edges of the remaining ponds and creeks.

Think of a web-footed guinea pig weighing a hundred pounds and you have the capybara, the world's largest rodent. In the lake country north of Manaus in Brazil or the watery wilderness of the Manu Wildlife Refuge in Peru, families of capybaras feed on aquatic plants such as water lilies, water hyacinths, and sedges. The animal's name translates as "master of the grasses."

Giant river otters may appear here as well. At five feet, they are the largest of the weasel family. Where there is one, there will be others, for they are social animals that hunt and play in family groups. Preferring clear water to hunt for fish and crustaceans, they are more often found in quiet lakes or in streams that drain upland rain forests. Opportunistic hunters, they will take water birds, caimans, and snakes, as well. When not dozing on fallen trees, they can be seen swimming like porpoises, arching gracefully out of the water to breathe and look about.

Another denizen of the rain forest's water world is tropical America's largest snake, the anaconda. Growing to nearly twenty feet in length and weighing well over two hundred pounds, it can capture even the rain forest's larger animals. Concealing itself close to shore amid aquatic plants, it waits at a spot where agoutis, capybaras, and tapirs come to drink. While the animal quenches its thirst, the snake grabs it and drags it into the water to drown. The anaconda's bite is powerful, but not poisonous.

Yellow
Anaconda
Eunectes notaeus

Like its much larger cousin, the gigantic green anaconda, the yellow anaconda will become aggressive if bothered. At home in water, on land, or in trees, the yellow anaconda captures young caimans, fish, frogs, turtles, rats, and birds that feed in or near water. Its generic name describes it as a good swimmer. Even at a length of seven to ten feet, the yellow anaconda is not large enough to be really dangerous as a constrictor and poses no threat to humans if left alone.

Yellow-spotted Amazon River Turtle

Podocnemis unifilis

Several species of sideneck turtles that have necks where their legs should be are common in the lowland rain forest, but their numbers are dwindling. Favoring the still waters of lakes, swamps, lagoons, and oxbows along the rivers of the major basins, members of this species sometimes exceed two feet in length. Only its cousin, the giant river turtle, grows larger. They feed mostly on vegetation. After mating in June or July, females travel far from the water to dig holes in the soil and lay their clutches of up to twenty-five eggs. Turtles excrete excess salt through tear ducts, or lachrymal glands, in their eye sockets. Here, a butterfly, alert for needed minerals, sips the salty fluid.

Anacondas are shy and not much of a threat to man, but every fisherman has an anaconda tale to tell. In 1990, for example, a lone fisherman, working his nets out of a canoe in Lake Acajituba north of Manaus, was seized by an adult anaconda, dragged overboard, and swallowed. Swollen with its huge meal, the snake could not swim easily and floated with the current into the Rio Negro. Passing fishermen, finding it there, caught and killed it. They took the serpent into Manaus to an office of Brazil's environmental agency where biologists opened up the stomach to recover the body of the unfortunate victim.

For some lowland rain forest creatures, such as the caiman, the dry season has both good and bad sides. Floating just under the water's surface with nothing showing but his bulging yellow eyes and prominent snorkel of a snout, the caiman waits for an insect, fingerling, or frog to happen by. With a lunge, he clamps down with his fifty conical teeth that pierce and grip, but don't chew, the victim. Under water, with the victim quite dead, the caiman swallows his catch with one convul-

sive gulp and delivers the meal to one of the most powerful digestive systems in nature.

Unfortunately for caimans, their diminished dry-season habitat exposes them to danger as well, as they must concentrate where hunters can find them. If a caiman is lucky, it might grow to a length of five to six feet. But at that size, it becomes a hunter's prize for its hide and meat. Each year, the skins of a million caimans enter the illegal international trade in reptile hides.

Similarly affected by changing habitat is the rain forest's largest predator and tropical America's largest cat, the jaguar. When rising waters force animals onto island refuges, the jaguar finds hunting easy. But when the dry season releases wildlife to range freely over newly exposed forests, the jaguar's task of catching a meal gets tougher.

A daytime hunter of deer, peccary, capybara, and even fish and caiman, this mottled stalker was revered by forest people as a powerful totem. "The sun created the jaguar to be his representative on earth," a Tucano Amazon Indian myth reveals.

Sulfur Butterflies
Phoebis sp.

These sulfur butterflies, photographed at a mineral lick near Brazil's Iguaçú Falls National Park, are members of the Pierinae family of a genus of white and yellow butterflies known as Phoebis. Sulfurs are often seen in large gatherings on damp ground where they sip mineral-rich water. Of the 20,000 species of butterflies in the world, half occur in the rain forests of tropical America. No part of the rain forest, from lowlands to highlands, is without its resident butterfly population. They play an important role in the reproduction of flowering plants, for which butterflies serve as vectors, taking pollen from one flower to another.

Tropical Rainstorm on the Napo River

Ecuador

Ocellated Turkey

Meleagris ocellata

As tropical Latin America's answer to the North American Thanksgiving bird, the ocellated turkey seems outfitted for a Carnaval parade. A little smaller than its domestic cousin, the ocellated turkey captivates with its blue head, metallic green and gold-barred body colors, blue and gold tail feathers, and pink legs. Nevertheless, ocellated turkeys are not easily seen, as they are extremely wary, preferring to feed in small family groups in dense deciduous thickets. Its species name "ocellata" refers to the red rings around its eyes.

Hunted for their gorgeous black and gold pelts, jaguars have been reduced in number to a few thousand individuals throughout their once wide range. They have learned to avoid settlements, even those of forest people. As *caboclos* (river people) press into the lowland rain forest following the canoe paths, jaguars abandon their favorite waterside haunts as well. They are seldom seen nowadays outside of national parks and forest reserves. Their preferred habitat has always been the dense lowland rain forest rather than the cloud forests.

Jaguar sightings often occur in the vicinity of streams or lakes. They enjoy stretching out on a sandbar to sun themselves, like big house cats. Even so, many native rain forest dwellers never see a jaguar in their entire lives.

More easily found are the many species of frogs that dwell mostly on the forest floor, away from the desiccating sun. Of the four thousand species of frogs in the world, perhaps a third are tropical tree frogs of many different genera. Perhaps the best known is the red-eyed tree frog, which has become the poster frog for rain forest conservation. Its huge

red-marble eyes stare out of countless magazine articles about nature, it seems. Also called the gaudy leaf frog, it relies on camouflage, quickness, and concealment (as opposed to poison) to avoid the bats, snakes, and raccoons that find it tasty.

Red Brocket Deer

Mazama americana

Small, shy creatures about half the size of a North American white-tailed deer, red brocket deer do well throughout the rain forest and in marshy grasslands despite constant pressure from hunters. Weighing from 50 to 100 pounds, brockets stand about two feet tall at the shoulder. They are well adapted to survival in the rain forest. Preferring dense thickets and swampy tangles, brockets feed on fruit, fallen flowers, mast, and fungi. Males have small unbranched antlers. In small family groups, they are able to hide in or escape through undergrowth too thick for most predators to pursue. When exposed at mineral licks, such as this one, watchfulness is the key to survival.

Ocelot

Leopardus pardalis

The beautiful markings of this small (twenty-pound) cat brought it to endangered species status in the previous decade, as hunters were killing up to 30,000 a year for their pelts. But given protection, the ocelot now maintains a presence throughout the rain forests of Latin America and as far north as Texas and Arizona. It is one of the most widespread of the felines, thanks to a wide prey base. Great jumpers and nimble climbers, ocelots are as at home in trees as on the ground. Entirely carnivorous, they take small mammals such as rats, opossums, and rabbits, but also snakes, lizards, and birds.

Brazilian Tapir
Tapirus terrestris

Tapirs claim several distinctions. They are the largest terrestrial mammals in the rain forest. They are the only New World representative of the hoofed mammals having an odd number of toes. And they have a flexible snout, not unlike that of an elephant. However, they are more closely related to horses and rhinoceroses. As big as a pony, an adult tapir can weigh more than 600 pounds. Night feeders, they forage beside and in rivers and lakes for the fruits, seeds, tubers, and leaves of most rain forest vegetation. The name *tapir* is of Indian origin.

Collared Peccary

Tayassu tajacu

Sometimes mistaken for wild pigs, peccaries are not actually members of the swine family. Their omnivorous feeding habits and adaptability have enabled them to survive throughout a wide rain forest range. Weighing up to sixty pounds and armed with formidable tusks, a mature peccary can become an adversary worthy of caution if disturbed. In groups numbering up to twenty, collared peccaries rummage the jungle floor for fruits, nuts, roots, and the foliage of many plants. Called *saino* in Spanish, they are identified by dozens of indigenous names, depending on the region.

Spectacled Bear

Tremarctos ornatus

Intensely shy and secretive, for good reason, the spectacled, or Andean, bear is threatened by hunting throughout his habitat of the Andes Cordillera. A smallish bear, an adult can reach a length of about five feet and height of around three feet at the shoulder. A healthy male of the species can weigh as much as 350 pounds. Females are smaller.

Farmers in Peru believe there are two species of spectacled bears, one that preys on livestock and another that eats crops. Actually, spectacled bears rely mostly on rain forest vegetation, climbing into trees to eat bromeliad hearts along with fruit, tender shoots, bulbs, and other vegetation.

Red-eyed Tree Frog
Agalychnis callidryas

Writing in *The Windward Road,* famed biologist Archie Carr explained why he found frogs so charming. "I like the look of frogs, and their outlook, and especially the way they get together in wet places on warm nights and sing about sex." Of rain forest frogs, none is better known than the diminutive red-eyed tree frog. The trademark eyes inspired its discoverer to name the genus after a scarlet flower. For the name of the species, he chose Latin words meaning "beautiful wood nymph."

Gold Frog
Brachycephalus ephippium

A survivor from the days of the dinosaur, the gold frog lives in the warm, moist coastal forest of eastern Brazil known as the Mata Atlantica, and nowhere else. Just three-quarters of an inch long, it is a primitive creature, having just two fingers on each hand and three toes on each foot. Like a toad, it inhabits the forest floor,

Yucatan Neotropical Rattlesnake

Crotalus durissus

The Central and South American tropics have but one pit viper, the neotropical rattlesnake also known as the cascabel. A heavy-bodied snake up to six feet long, it is usually found in dry upland forests or in grasslands, where it feeds on small mammals and large lizards. As do all pit vipers, the neotropical rattlesnake has a heat-sensing organ located in two pits on either side of its head, enabling it to strike accurately in the dark. The generic name *Crotalus* comes from a Greek word for "a rattle." The local name *cascabel* comes from a Spanish word for "small bell."

Tayra

Eira barbara

Found throughout the entire Amazon Basin, this little member of the weasel family hunts the forest floor for small mammals and insects, but just as readily climbs into the understory in search of birds, insects, fruit, and beehives, which it will raid. Weighing up to fifteen pounds, the tayra is strong and tough, routinely hunting in the daytime over many square miles of territory. A solitary creature, it is often mistaken for the bush dog and looks much like a large, sturdy mink. Its name is of Indian origin.

Jaguar
Panthera onca

The rain forest's largest predator, the jaguar ranks at the top of Indian mythology, and the food chain, as "the beast that kills its prey with one leap." Where once the jaguar ranged as far north as Texas, its habitat is now confined largely to remote rain forests.

Surprisingly, for an animal that can weigh up to 300 pounds, the jaguar can hunt in trees or water or on land with equal ease. It enjoys a broad prey base that can include capybara, peccary, and deer on land, and giant otter, tapir, caiman, and fish in its aquatic domain.

Central American Agouti
Dasyprocta punctata

Every forest meat eater hunts this reddish brown rodent that is sometimes called the Indian rabbit. Nevertheless, its ability to hide in thick brush helps it survive throughout the Central American rain forest. A relative of the guinea pig, the Central American agouti weighs between seven and ten pounds. It feeds during the day, usually alone, on seeds, fruit, flowers, and insects. Its habit of burying nuts as food reserves helps distribute these seeds and spread the growth of forest trees. Although they mate for life, male and female agoutis travel separately, perhaps as a survival strategy.

Brazilian Porcupine
Coendou prehensilis

Although Brazilian porcupines have a dozen or more relatives all over South and Central America, they are the most widespread and numerous of all the porcupine family. Slow moving and secretive, they depend on concealment for protection, but they can move swiftly if necessary and can climb trees as well as a squirrel. Feeding at night, these tree-dwelling mammals are vegetarians, eating fruit, nuts, leaves, and tree bark. The spines that guard their heads and bodies are long, sharp, and dangerous, with barbs that keep them from falling out once embedded.

Bush Dog

Speothus venaticus

Unimpressive little creatures, bush dogs are among the few canids to have evolved in tropical America and are now quite rare in their Amazon Basin range. With short legs and tail, and long, narrow body, the average adult bush dog weighs just ten to fifteen pounds. Small packs of four to seven animals hunt mainly at night. To escape capture, pacas often submerge in water, so bush dogs, too, have learned to dive in and swim under-water in pursuit. The Latin generic name combines two words of Greek origin that translate as "cave" and "jackal"; the species name means "hunter."

Giant River Otter

Pteronura brasiliensis

Large animals, giant otters approach a length of four feet and weigh around sixty pounds when mature. Their range extends throughout the Amazon Basin, wherever sizable lakes and rivers provide habitat and food supply. Their generic name describes their flattened tails that aid in swimming. Families of up to a dozen giant otters stay close together, both to hunt and for protection against large predators, such as jaguars. Once shot by hunters for their pelts and by competing fishermen, giant otter numbers sank to endangered status in previous decades. With protection, they are coming back.

When army ants spread a phalanx across the rain forest floor, motmots follow closely, gobbling up grasshoppers, beetles, and lizards fleeing the implacable ants. With strong, saw-edged beaks, motmots can kill and cut up creatures as large as a mouse. At other times, motmots perch and swing their long, pendulous tails while waiting for prey to appear. A motmot pair makes a nest by tunneling into a clay bank. There, parents take turns incubating their eggs. The common name *motmot* is of Mexican origin and describes their call, which is a soft, two-note "woop-oop."

Broad-billed Motmot
Electron platyrhynchum

Capped Heron
Pilherodius pileatus

A small and graceful bird living only in the Latin American rain forests, the capped heron feeds by prowling the edges of forested rivers for minnows, tadpoles, and crustaceans. It grows to a height of about twenty inches. From a distance, this light-colored heron could be mistaken for one of its close relatives among the egrets, but up close, its bright blue face and black cap with white tassel become evident. The name, *pileatus,* calls attention to its crest.

Double-crested Basilisk

Basiliscus plumifrons

The huge and monstrous basilisk of medieval legend could kill with a look, but these slender, colorful members of the iguana family just have the looks. Up to thirty inches in length, the tree-dwelling basilisk of the lowland rain forest relies on the long, splayed toes of its hind legs to stand up and scamper across water surfaces at speeds of up to seven miles an hour to escape predators such as snakes or raccoons. Basilisks feed on insects, frogs, and fish that they find in their preferred habitat beside the shores of lakes and rivers.

Caiman
Caiman crocodilus

Throughout the lowland rain forest basins, wherever lakes and streams furnish quiet water, caimans sun themselves on the banks during the day. At night, these smallest of the American crocodiles float quietly with only their periscope eyes protruding above the surface, alert for frogs, fish, and aquatic insects. Both parents look after their eggs and help the little ones into the water when they hatch. Seldom more than three feet in length, caimans fall prey to jaguars, anacondas, large wading birds, foxes, black crocodiles, and humans. Hide hunters take them for the manufacture of shoes, purses, and wallets.

Mountain Paca
Agouti taczanowskii

Related to the agouti, or paca, of the lowland rain forests, the mountain paca is seriously endangered through loss of its habitat in the forests of the Andes Mountains of Ecuador, Peru, Colombia, and northwestern Venezuela. Regarded as tasty by carnivores of all kinds, this hare-sized rodent relies on fecundity as a survival mechanism. Females can and do reproduce throughout the year. Giving frequent birth to large litters, they are able to sustain their numbers. Populations of the little known mountain paca appear to be declining, though, as their mountainside homes are deforested for valuable timber.

2 : the understory

Cockle-shell Orchid

Beneath the sunlit rain forest canopy overhead and above the leaf-strewn forest floor below, the understory spreads out as an environmental stratum possessed of its own specialized floral and faunal life forms.

Dendrologists—people who study trees and shrubs—argue over what constitutes an understory, or even if there is such a thing. But most of the technical literature suggests that in contrast to the two-layered forests of temperate zones, tropical forests appear to have three or even more strata, each with its own identity. As do the rain forests themselves, understories differ in character with location, elevation, temperature averages, cloud cover, and the availability of nutrients. In the higher elevations, such as in the montane rain forests, tree height

dwindles. In the rarefied air of ten thousand feet, where cool temperatures and enveloping clouds affect growing conditions, miniature elfin rain forest trees grow no more than head high and the understory consists mostly of ferns and mosses.

While canopy trees of lowland rain forests soar one hundred and twenty feet before unfolding their leafy parasols to the open sky, trees of the understory seldom grow to half that height, usually from thirty to sixty feet. Most are evergreen, never shedding their broad, light-collecting leaves. Of the five hundred species of trees that taxonomists have identified in rain forests, two-thirds find their environmental niche in the understory or subcanopy.

In this natural sauna, protected from sun and wind, surrounded by watery air, epiphytic plants—especially orchids and bromeliads—flourish. Taking root in the crotches of trees and along the tops of large branches, they capture moisture with their dangling velamen-clad roots and soak up nutrients oozing down the bark surfaces of their host trees. Ingeniously adaptive bromeliads store their drinking water in hollow rosettes formed by their long leathery leaves. Frogs and insects live in these little cisterns.

In all rain forest environments, tree ferns and mosses flourish on every horizontal surface, often furnishing an anchoring base for other types of epiphytic plants. A single understory tree can play host to scores of different plant species, which in turn play host to dozens

Wedge-capped Capuchin Monkey
Cebus olivaceus

Also known as the weeping capuchin because of the black widow's peak of its cap, this monkey is common in Venezuela, northeastern Brazil, and the Guianas. Weighing from five to ten pounds and equipped with a long, prehensile tail, wedge-capped capuchins search the middle and lower levels of the forest for food. Not fussy eaters, they feed on seeds, flowers, fruits, insects, small animals, and birds, almost anything edible. They gather in groups of up to thirty or more and observe a distinct dominance hierarchy. Young nursing mothers, for example, must allow older females of higher rank to nurse. This youngster was photographed in Canaima National Park in Venezuela.

Spotted Orchid

Monteverde Cloud Forest
Costa Rica

of flying, creeping, and crawling creatures that rely on them for food and shelter.

While understory animal life can't compete in numbers and variety with that of the canopy, it is richer in certain forms. For example, Latin America's forty-nine species of tropical monkeys call the understory home, along with scores of other tree-dwelling mammals.

One good reason is the prevalence of food. Sheltered from the withering sun, many flowering and fruit-bearing trees do well in the understories of lowland and montane rain forests. Their nectaries and fruits, such as figs, bananas, mangos, papayas, pineapples, guava, bread-

fruits, cacao, and coffee serve up a convenience store for small animals.

Butterflies and moths, able to fly easily through the open spaces of the subcanopy, thrive in tropical America, which counts about half of the world's twenty thousand species of these colorful insects. Lepidopterists record new species every year. Butterflies of many species gather by the thousands on sandbars or gravel banks near streams to sip water. The neon blue morphos can't be missed, but a close look at what appears to be a dry, brown leaf may reveal one of the leaf-mimic butterflies. Its cunning imitation recreates a dead leaf, even to the point of faking the nibbles of a caterpillar along the edges of its wings.

Highly specialized crawlers, such as the thirty-seven species of leaf-cutter ants, gather the leaves of understory trees and shrubs. Cutting each leaf into bits, the ants carry the leaf pieces back to their colonies as nourishment for their only food, a highly specialized fungus grown in their underground farms.

Other crawlers are there, as well. Cunningly camouflaged snakes slither aloft along lianas and stranglers attached to the forest giants in their nightly hunt for food. Using heat sensors, they locate small warm creatures such as tree rats or birds, which they kill and eat. They find cold-blooded frogs and lizards by means of olfactory organs in their tongues that smell the prey and pinpoint its location.

Twenty-six species of marsupial opossums, from the tiny mouse opossum to the relatively large Virginia opossum, feed omnivorously on subcanopy flora and fauna. Several small cats, such as the margay, jaguarundi, and oncilla, hunt opossums in turn, as well as rats, mice, and roosting birds.

The tiny silky anteater investigates understory tree branches for ants and termites that, in their millions, make the arboreal habitat their home. An adult silky anteater may consume up to five thousand ants a day, breaking into their nests and licking up the residents as they emerge. Its thick soft coat of fur keeps it safe from bites and stings. When day breaks, the little creature anchors itself in the crotch of a tree, curls up in a ball no bigger than a grapefruit, and goes to sleep.

Forty species of arboreal rodents, tree rats and tree mice large and small, find refuge in the understory's rich environment. Eighteen species of bats rely on the understory for shelter during the day, when

Colubrid Snake
Colubridae spp.

Tropical rain forests, with their huge populations of small animals, have appropriately large populations of small snakes that feed upon this prey base. Disguised in greens or browns or mottled in camouflage colors to resemble vines, lianas, and tree leaves, snakes of the Colubrid family are much in evidence. They offer little danger to humans, although some members are mildly poisonous. They prowl the forest floor and its lower levels for rats, birds, lizards, and especially frogs. Nabbed, the prey is squeezed to death and then slowly swallowed.

they hang suspended from branches in dim recesses, inside leaf "tents," or within tree hollows. They share their space with twelve species of arboreal porcupines that forage the middle stratum for fruit, leaves, and tree bark.

With few exceptions, monkeys spend most of their lives in the understory, climbing into the canopy only when trees are fruiting or descending to the ground when nuts ripen and fall. Packs of little squirrel monkeys, commonplace in the middle and lowland rain forests, clamber noisily through the trees. They savor the beetles, grasshoppers, and caterpillars that they find around cultivated crops of fruits and nuts, so they are often seen around human habitation. Troops of them can be seen swinging from branch to branch while chattering and calling like a flock of birds.

Much larger spider monkeys range throughout the lowland forests and into the lower hillsides, swinging wildly through the branches with the aid of long, slender arms and legs and a prehensile tail. Heavily hunted by forest people as food, spider monkeys have learned to almost never leave the safety of the trees for the perilous ground. One of their number, the woolly spider monkey, also known as the muriqui, is listed as endangered. Though it is no longer hunted as food, its continued existence is threatened by habitat loss. An estimated 85 percent of the coastal rain forests of southeastern Brazil, where the muriqui lives, has been deforested for agriculture and development.

Howler monkeys, once heard, never forgotten, make both lowland and montane rain forests their home. Families of howlers keep in touch with each other by means of low-pitched roars of several seconds' duration, followed by coughing grunts. Their cries carry for miles, and are usually answered by relatives living some distance away. In the wild, howlers usually check in with each other in early morning and late afternoon. (Those in the Houston Zoo no longer call at the start of day, but routinely respond to the roars of leaf-blowers used to clear paths of debris.)

Red Howler Monkey
Alouatta seniculus

Most widespread of the howler monkeys, the red howler occupies most of the Amazon Basin and most of South America east of the Andes Mountains. Covered with reddish fur, they are big, robust monkeys that form large families of up to sixty individuals. They like mature rain forest habitat where the trees are large enough for them to travel on the branches easily. Possessed of an enlarged throat sac, males vocalize with sustained, deep-toned roars that carry for miles. Although not endangered, red howler numbers are down, as they are heavily hunted by forest people for their tasty meat.

Cock-of-the-Rock

Rupicola peruviana

A dominant male cock-of-the-rock takes a stance on his jungle throne and defies his rivals with an aggressive snarl. Contenders gather, hoping to displace him as the mate of a drably hued female. A suitor occupies a branch near the master of the lek and flashes his brilliant red-orange feathers. The dominant male responds with leaps and flutters. A raucous vocal hullabaloo ensues. After an hour of hopeful whooping and posturing, the challengers depart, and the dominant male joins his rarely seen female, shown here feeding her chick.

Howler monkeys and their woolly cousins rest and sleep in favorite trees at lower levels, climbing into the canopy during the day to find fruits, nuts, flowers, and young leaves.

Capuchins, found in all rain forest habitats, are thought to be the smartest of the New World primates, surviving by caution, cleverness, and adaptability. They crack open palm nuts by whacking them against branches, eat tender buds, birds' eggs, and any small creature they can catch and tear apart.

Less adaptable and far more threatened are the nineteen species of diminutive marmosets and tamarin monkeys that live in the coastal rain forests of Brazil. Their chief handicap is that they are small and cute, and thus valued as pets. In addition, they have been unable to adapt to the near total loss of their accustomed coastal habitat. Acknowledging the problem, the Brazilian government recently took steps to protect one of the rarest of their species by setting aside a reserve for the golden lion tamarin in a fragment of coastal rain forest northeast of Rio de Janeiro.

For owls, whose silent flight and visual acuity work to their advantage, the understory is an ideal place to pounce on tree-climbing rodents, small monkeys, and lizards. Woodpeckers drill for grubs hidden beneath the bark of the forest giants. In montane rain forests and cloud forests, the understory is the preferred habitat of some of the world's most spectacular birds, such as the cock-of-the-rock.

Ranked by many at the very top of the bird beauty pageant, the male Andean cock-of-the-rock sports colors of red, blue-gray, and black that would stop traffic. His most distinguishing feature is the

nimbus of feathers that covers his head and beak in a disk that extends from nape to throat. His round yellow eye peers out of this scarlet powder puff well back of the point where logic suggests it should be. In the dim, damp understory of his Andean cloud forest habitat, the appearance of this pigeon-sized bird commands attention, especially that of the drab, shy females whose favors the males seek. One cock-of-the-rock lek, or courtship ground, in the Peruvian cloud forest is said to be the largest in tropical America. It stays in use much of the year. When mating fever reaches its peak in August, twelve or more males sometimes compete within its small area for up to four females, creating an uproar of astonishing volume.

Curiously, the mammals and birds of this habitat rely on just 1 percent of the understory trees for 80 percent of the fruit, nuts, and nectar that they eat. Trees and plants so vital to the survival of many creatures are known to biologists as keystone species, because entire ecosystems would fail without them. To study the health of rain forests, biologists keep track of keystone species in an effort to gauge the condition of the forest as a whole.

One research technique employs an examination of the relationship of orchids and their pollinators, a group of bees in the Euglossine family known as the orchid bees. These are small stingless bees that nest in holes in trees or in underground burrows. Colorful in metallic gold and green, they look as if they had been crafted by a goldsmith for a Russian czarina. As keystone species, Euglossine bees pollinate some 650 species of orchids.

When orchids bloom, as they do throughout the year in the rain forest, bees gather their nectar and simultaneously

Common Marmoset

Callithrix jacchus

Tiny forest gnomes no larger than the leaves they hide behind, marmosets seem more like sprites than monkeys. Just eight or nine inches long, weighing little more than a half-pound, marmosets remain fairly common in the lowland rain forest, perhaps because they are too small to be worth the price of a shotgun shell. The tufted-ear marmoset, also known as the common marmoset, feeds on fruits, nuts, and tree sap. Using a lower jaw with special chisel-shaped teeth, he gnaws holes in tree bark and licks up the juices that collect there. Mutual grooming is important to marmosets, and they spend hours at this favorite pastime.

pollinate the flowers. In time, the orchid seed pods burst and release millions of tiny seeds to be spread by wind and rainwater. If there are suitable trees nearby, some of the seeds find a spot to take root and grow. As the seedlings mature and bloom, their blossoms provide food for yet more bees. But if trees are cut down, the orchids they once supported can no longer sustain life. With fewer orchids and their bee-sustaining nectar, there will be fewer bees. Thus a check on the keystone bee populations should provide an advance warning that their ecosystem is in trouble. Conversely, a thriving bee population should confirm the health of a stable or growing forest.

Any threat to a keystone species worries scientists concerned with healthy rain forests. For the rest of us, who require breathable air, drinkable water, palatable food, and effective medicines, rain forests are the keystone in the architecture of world health.

Cayambe-Coca Reserve

Ecuador

Acorn Woodpecker

Melanerpes formicivorous

Found in the montane rain forest and usually around oak trees, the acorn woodpecker feeds on acorns, storing away spare nuts for the off-season in holes it drills in tree bark. It also catches insects on the fly and often drops to the forest floor to feast on ants. Groups of up to twelve birds share the same territory and defend it against intruders. The bird's generic name means "black creeper"; the species name translates as "ant eating."

Crimson-crested Woodpecker

Campephilus melanoleucos

There's no mistaking this big bird with the all-red head for anything other than the prototypical woodpecker. Fourteen inches from beak to tail, *Campephilus* bears a strong resemblance to several close cousins, all sharing much the same feeding and nesting habits. Inhabiting both upland and lowland rain forests, this woodpecker drills into the bark of trees in search of insect larvae. Pairs nest in cavities chiseled into dead trees, usually twenty feet or more above ground. The generic name reveals that it "likes caterpillars."

Yellow-bellied Elaenia

Elaenia flavogaster

Ranging from the lowlands to the high-lands, this six-inch songster is a conspicuous resident of the rain forest. Mated pairs sing together, although their duets lack a discernible melody. They cooperate in building a nest, with the male hauling in twigs and grass to create a cup with sides turned in so that the two eggs cannot roll out. Like other flycatchers, the adults feed on insects usually caught in midair, but they also consume fruit and seeds.

Jaguarundi

Herpailurus yaguarondi

Should you see a cat in the rain forest, chances are it will be this one, but you may mistake it for a weasel. With its flat head and small ears, long sleek body, short legs, gray to reddish brown fur, and small size (twelve to twenty-two pounds) the jaguarundi looks more like a weasel than its feline relations. Widely distributed throughout South and Central America, this small prowler searches the ground and in the understory for mammals, birds, and snakes. Its name, of Greek origin, describes a creeping animal.

Coati

Nasua narica

Like its cousin the raccoon in North America, the coati occupies a broad niche in the tropical rain forests east of the Andes Mountains. Coati is a South American Indian word; the Latin name, *Nasua narica,* refers to its long, mobile snout. Daytime feeders, coatis are at home in almost any habitat, foraging on the ground or climbing through the trees like squirrels. Their food includes fruits, nuts, insects, birds' eggs, and lizards. They reach a length of around four feet, including their long tails, and can weigh up to thirteen pounds.

Leaf Frog
Phyllomedusa vaillanti

Cousin to the red-eyed tree frog, the leaf frog lacks red eyes, but boasts purple shorts. Less than an inch long, the leaf frog inhabits rain forest trees near swamps and ponds, where it feeds at night on insects. Breeding takes place in a bush by the water. The female lays her several hundred eggs on a leaf, which she then folds over to hide them. Hatching tadpoles drop into the water below. During the day they cluster in a school, but disperse at night in search of food. After maturing, the young leaf frog returns to its arboreal habitat.

Forest Fakers

To survive in a rain forest filled with insatiable appetites, animals need an edge, a way to escape a predator's jaws. Among insects, for example, disguising oneself as something carnivores don't eat—a leaf, a twig, a lichen—provides the edge. Scientists call this type of protective adaptation *crypsis,* or cryptic coloration. The leaf-mimic butterfly, for example, hangs from a twig with wings folded, cunningly camouflaged, even to the color and skeletal veining of the real leaf it copies. When sipping moisture from wet sand, it presses its

Leaf-mimic Praying Mantis
Choerododis strumaria

wings together and avoids movement while other more colorful drinkers continually open and close their wings. The leaf-mimic praying mantis, a brown, sticklike creature in other manifestations, has transformed itself into a green leaf look-alike and hides in full view on a leaf of the same color and pattern. Abandoning green, the leaf-mimic katydid assumes the appearance of a dead leaf, wrinkled and brown, with the mimicry enhanced by stains and holes as if the leaf had been chewed by a katydid. As their cryptic coloration of choice, two species of grasshoppers have chosen mosses and lichens, among the most common of all plant forms in the rain forest. Their legs and bodies sprout green leaflike spikes characteristic of their host plants. The stick-mimic grasshopper, in contrast, makes itself a dead-ringer for a twig so as to fool a hungry motmot in search of a meal. Many life forms use *crypsis* to enhance hunting success or avoid detection by hunters. But few accomplish such clever transformations as do insects.

Leaf-mimic Butterfly
Aenea panariste

Leaf-mimic Katydid
Typophyllum mortuifolium

Stick-mimic Grasshopper
Utropidacris cristata

Moss-mimic Grasshopper
Tettigoniidae spp.

Lichen-mimic Grasshopper
Tettigoniidae spp.

Mexican Black Howler Monkey
Alouatta pigra

In just a few remaining lowland areas of Belize and the Yucatan peninsula, Mexican black howler monkeys still fill the twilight air with their strange roars and coughs. But not for long, if clearing of forest lands for farms and ranches continues at the present pace. Listed as endangered, they are among the largest of the New World monkeys, with males as big as a middle-sized dog. They differ from their cousins in that both sexes are black, but like other howlers, live largely on fruits and leaves. These are the monkeys that tourists see around archaeological sites, where they are safe from hunters.

Tropical America hosts six different species of howler monkeys, all sharing many of the same physical characteristics, but differing in various ways. They are the noisiest of all rain forest monkeys. A male howler possesses a pocket below his chin which acts as a resonating chamber to add volume to the bass roar generated in a modified larynx. The call, a sustained hoot followed by a series of coughs, can be heard for miles. Slow-moving and sedentary, brown howler monkeys feed mostly on vegetation, eating leaves and tender shoots, along with fruit and flowers.

Brown Howler Monkey
Alouatta fusca

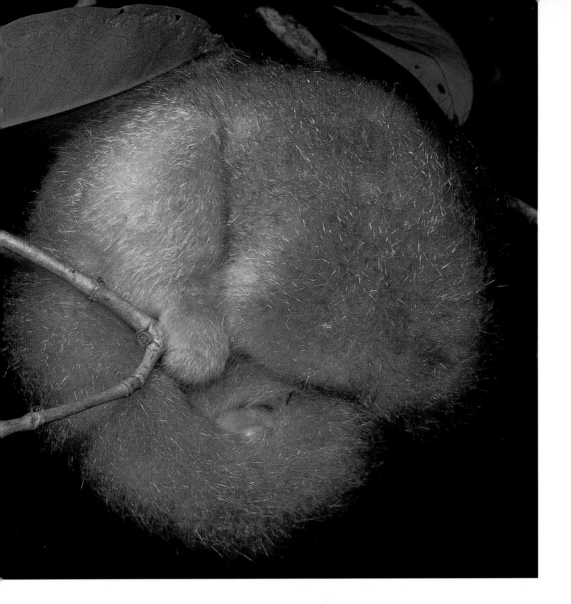

Silky Anteater

Cyclopes didactylus

Seldom seen, little known, the silky anteater works the night shift as a creature of the understory and sleeps the day away. When darkness comes, this tiny arboreal mammal uncoils from his perch in a lowland rain forest tree and sets out to hunt for ants, from which he is protected by his dense fur. While his prehensile tail helps him climb, he relies more on the curved claws on his toes to move around on vines and tree limbs. Weighing no more than half a pound, he is sometimes called the "little angel."

Tent-making Bats
brown: *Uroderma bilobatum*
white: *Ectophylla alba*

Lacking caves and other suitable shelter, several of the rain forest's many bat species have learned to use the broad leaves of certain rain forest plants as tents. As many as fifty tent-makers such as *Uroderma bilobatum*, above, may cling toe-to-toe to the underside of a banana leaf which they have prepared by cutting along the central rib to make the sides droop down. Feeders on fruit, flower nectar, and insects, these tent-makers range from Mexico south to Bolivia and southeastern Brazil.

Another tent-making bat is *Ectophylla alba,* which looks like a white mouse with wings. This tiny nighttime fruiteater weighs just one and a half ounces. A rare and unusual species, it is one of the few bats that is all white. Groups of bats make themselves a roost by biting holes along the midrib of a *Heliconia* leaf so that the sides of the leaf fold down. Then they snuggle together inside their tent to wait out the day.

Guira Cuckoo

Guira guira

Always found in small flocks of up to ten, guira cuckoos roost together (closely ranked on the same tree branch), feed together (usually hunting on the ground for worms, insects, and lizards), and nest together. As communal nesters, several females will build one nest, lay their eggs in it, take turns incubating them, and when the chicks hatch, share the feeding chores. Unlike other species of cuckoos, the Indian-named guiras do not lay their eggs in other birds' nests.

Brown Titi Monkey
Callicebus moloch

From within a dense bamboo thicket, pairs of brown titis greet the dawn with a piercing duet of whoops and shrieks of amazing volume. With the sun welcomed, these leaf-eating monkeys feed together in small family groups on bamboo and other foliage as the only monkey species to subsist largely on leaves. Residents of the lowland rain forests of the Amazon Basin, brown titis weigh only two to three pounds and range up to eighteen inches tall. Their tails are as long as their bodies, enabling them to feed with both hands while hanging suspended from a branch.

Woolly Spider Monkey
Brachyteles arachnoides

Brazilian coastal rain forests harbor the largest of tropical America's monkeys, the endangered woolly spider monkey, or muriqui. Weighing upwards of thirty pounds and with body lengths of thirty inches, muriquis are so highly evolved for their habitat that they have lost the thumbs on their hands. In exchange, perhaps, they have gained long prehensile tails so strong that their owners can hang from the underside of tree branches with them. Leaf eaters, muriquis like the fruits and flowers of various trees as well.

Owl Monkey

Aotus trivirgatus

Also known as the night monkey, this is the world's only nocturnal primate. With huge, light-gathering eyes set close together, it can see in the dark. Lacking a prehensile tail, the owl monkey prefers to creep along branches on all fours with its long, black-tipped tail hanging straight down, but it can and does leap from branch to branch. Small groups of up to a half-dozen feed quietly in the understory on leaves, flowers, and small animals, communicating only with soft, owl-like hoots. Adult males reach a weight of two to three pounds; females are smaller. Subspecies of the Aotus family are common in most tropical rain forest habitats east of the Andes and in Central America.

Leaf-cutter Ants
Atta cephalotes

As an example of a highly organized society, that of the leaf-cutter ants has few peers. The specialized members of a leaf-cutter ant colony may number as many as five million individuals occupying an underground nest 150 feet in diameter. Media workers, as they are called, climb trees and bushes to clip away bits of leaves, which they bring back to nourish their fungus gardens. Other workers clean and scrape the leaves and chew them into a sticky ball composed of saliva combined with feces. As a type of fungus spreads on this material, ants feed on its growing tips.

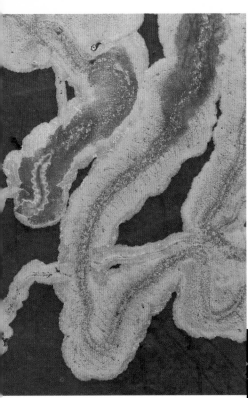

Common Morpho Butterfly
Morpho peleides

The fluorescent blue flash of a morpho butterfly's wings as it soars and bobs down a jungle path is a true highlight of any visit to the rain forest. Lighting to feed, the mor-

Leaf Miner
unknown species

Leaf miners by the hundreds of species thrive in the rain forest, with its banquet of bushes and trees. A typical leaf miner, in its adult form, is a small, nondescript butterfly that lays its eggs on the leaves of a preferred tree. Tiny flat larvae hatching from the eggs burrow into the host leaf and feed on its inner tissue. The burrowing larvae excavate chambers within the leaf alongside its ribs where they turn into pupae and remain safe from predation. Emerging as adult insects, the winged miners mate and find new leaves on which to lay their eggs.

pho closes its wings and displays on the undersides eyespots intended to discourage hungry predators. With wingspans of four to five inches, the *Morpho* genus of eighty species includes some of the world's largest butterflies. While not yet endangered, their numbers have been reduced by professional butterfly hunters.

Glass Frog
Centrolenella

Tiny glass frogs are smaller than a 25-cent piece and almost transparent. They make diligent parents. A gravid female searches out a bush or tree with branches that hang over a pond or stream of water, chooses a protected place on the underside of a broad leaf, and lays her eggs there in a jellylike mass. The male fertilizes them, and then guards the clutch, staying nearby to protect the eggs from insects and parasites. When the tadpoles hatch, they fall (or are pushed) out of the jelly into the water below.

Hoatzin

Opisthocomus hoazin

A giant cuckoo wearing blue eye shadow and a fright wig, the hoatzin looks like a reincarnation of *Archaeopteryx,* a prototypical bird of the Mesozoic Age. Hoatzin chicks are hatched with claws on their wings that they use in crawling around in trees. Found in rain forests near the margins of lakes and rivers, the hoatzin can eat the leaves of plants that other birds find toxic, thanks to a foregut where the material is fermented with microorganisms. This digestive process generates an offensive odor that transmits to the bird's flesh so that forest people call them "stink birds" and leave them alone.

Though resembling an oversized humming-bird, the colorful jacamar feeds entirely on insects. Always found in pairs, jacamars wait on a perch in the understory to dash out and grab passing bugs, which they swallow whole. Butterflies are rendered edible by first knock-ing off the insect's wings. For a nest, the jacamar couple burrows into the side of a clay bank, taking turns digging out a foot-deep tube, where the female lays two eggs. As they excavate their hideaway, the male sings his most melodious songs.

Rufous-tailed Jacamar
Galbula ruficauda

White-faced Capuchin Monkey

Cebus capucinus

Also called the white-throated capuchin, these medium-sized monkeys range throughout Central America and parts of northwestern South America. Family groups of up to twenty-four members forage noisily for fruit, nuts, and insects, which they find by examining the undersides of leaves and by peeling away bark from tree limbs. The tips of their tails are prehensile, enabling them to hold on to branches for safety while using their hands to feed. Daytime feeders, white-faced capuchins live in all rain forest habitats from montane to lowland. Not heavily hunted, they are nevertheless threatened by loss of habitat, as deforestation makes inroads into their territories.

3 : the canopy

Resplendent Quetzal

Pharomachrus mocinno

Sacred to the Maya and the national bird of Guatemala, the quetzal is admired by many as one of the most beautiful birds in the world. A dove-sized bird with tail feathers two feet long, the locally endangered quetzal's range is limited largely to Central America and southern Mexico, where it needs undisturbed hillsides of montane rain forests and cloud forests. Fruit, lizards, frogs, and insects compose its diet. Birders regard a quetzal sighting as a major coup, but few have seen its most dramatic performance, staged during mating season. The male flies to the topmost limits of the canopy, circles and sings, then plummets straight down, tail feathers streaming.

Tree canopies in the rain forest sustain prodigious numbers of insects, lizards, birds, and mammals. Biologists have known this for decades, but only in recent years has technology given them the equipment and associated technology needed to observe and understand the creatures living high in the canopy.

Today, scientists use tower cranes, cherry pickers, extension ladders, bosun's chairs, capstan winches, aerial trams, tree bicycles, walkways, helicopters, ultralight aircraft, and blimps to gain direct observation of canopy life. Using fine-meshed nets, stupefying chemical fog, gas, smoke, mechanical shakers, thrashers, and traps, they have uncovered a world so heavily populated as to astound even the most hopeful of specialists. They estimate that forest canopies may shelter as many as 100 million different species of arthropods, chiefly ants, beetles, and spiders. That's two hundred times the known density of marine invertebrates. And that doesn't count all the other creatures populating the canopy: snails, mites, lizards, frogs, birds, and small mammals that eat arthropods or graze on tree leaves.

Of nearly four thousand species of birds native to the American tropics, most depend on the forest canopy as home and breadbasket. For casual visitors and experts alike, they are difficult to see. Toucans, with their huge banana-shaped bills and gaudy colors, should be as obvious as a stoplight, yet they seem to disappear into the canopy's foliage. Only their hoarse gargling cries give them away. Some small drab birds, such as the screaming piha, almost defy discovery within their leafy apartments, although their ventriloquial calls echo incessantly through the canopy.

More visible are some of the 322 species of dazzling hummingbirds that whiz erratically among the canopy's flowers, drinking nectar. Thirty-nine species of trogons, the show-offs of the rain forest world,

gather the canopy's fruits and nuts. The most resplendent of their number is the quetzal, arguably the gaudiest of all, with its brilliant feathers
in green, gold, and red, bottomed off with long tail plumes. The Maya
and Aztec people revered the quetzal as sacred, and treasured its tail
plumes as priestly decorations. Another canopy resi-
dent is the bellbird, which sits in the crown of the
tallest tree and advertises its presence with a gong-
like call that carries for miles.

Far more numerous are the energetic flycatchers
that swarm the canopy's upper reaches along with the
hummingbirds that sip the nectar of epiphytes flowering on high. Small and quick, they are difficult to
study. Scientists catch them with nets suspended in a
gap or corridor cut between canopy trees or raised like
a square-rigged sail in natural openings. Captured
birds are painlessly examined, weighed, and mea-
sured. A tiny blood sample is taken. Then they are
released unharmed, having added a bit to the mosaic
of knowledge about canopy life.

For birds of many kinds, the canopy is irre-
placeable. Yet scientists observe that reliable scientific
knowledge of how birds use the canopy and its food
base is almost completely lacking.

Green parrots—short and chunky—stream over-
head in flocks, chattering noisily to each other. Settling
into the upper reaches of the tallest trees, perhaps 180
feet up, they crawl over the branches to pluck flowers
and fruit.

Their larger cousins, the multicolored macaws—long and slender—wheel in slow, ponderous flight over canopy trees in search of

El Yunque Rain Forest

Puerto Rico

Hyacinth Macaw

Anodorhynchus hyacinthinus

At a length of almost three feet, the hyacinth macaw is among the largest of the parrots. Its spectacular looks make it popular as a pet, and its affinity for palm groves makes it relatively easy to find and capture. As a consequence, hyacinth macaws are classified as a threatened species. Preferring a habitat near water, they are believed to nest high in the tops of the tallest trees. A truly massive bill enables the bird to cut through the tough shells of palm and other nuts as well as the seeds of various fruits. The bill, which is unnotched, is noted in its generic name, which means "toothless" or "smooth beak."

palm nuts. With powerful shears for beaks, they crush the tough palm nuts into nourishing pulp.

Together, parrots and macaws seem like the quintessential tropical rain forest birds. When they burst from the top of a kapok tree in a blaze of color and noise, one gets the kind of show expected of a rain forest. Yet macaw and parrot numbers are dwindling, in some cases, almost to the vanishing point. Habitat loss may have the most serious and lasting impact. Deforestation simply removes the nest trees they must have to reproduce, along with the fruit- and nut-bearing trees that are their food source. Each additional acre of rain forest that is cut down reduces the habitat available to the animals that live in it. Not surprisingly, forty-two species of parrots are thought to be close to extinction.

Two methods offer promise in ongoing studies of canopy birds. Larger birds such as eagles, vultures, guans, and hornbills can be tracked by satellite telemetry. A tiny transmitter fastened to the bird's back broadcasts its location to a satellite in space, which in turn relays the information to a monitor below. As a rule, the transmitter must weigh no more than 3 percent of the bird's body weight, limiting it to the largest of the canopy birds. Macaws and parrots are too small for satellite tracking.

Researchers equip smaller birds with a tiny radio transmitter no bigger than a pencil eraser and follow its signal from an ultralight airplane. Ultralights have proven to be a safe, effective, adaptable, and relatively inexpensive tool. They are quiet and slow, and birds don't fear them.

For long-term study around permanent base camps, researchers build walkways and platforms high in the canopy. With easy access, observers can spend hours or days in observation.

The same arrangement allows biologists to study the twelve orders of mammals that use the forest canopy, both as grazers of the

vegetation and as predators of its resident prey base. One survey tabulated a total of seventy-eight species of nonflying mammals, including animals such as monkeys, marsupials, rodents, and three carnivores, including the kinkajou and the margay. In addition, the survey tabulated forty-two species of bats.

Some frog species of the many that inhabit the canopy have developed poison as an effective defense against predation. Herpetologists say that all frogs possess a degree of poison in the juices that moisten their skins. A few secrete poisons that are truly lethal. In fact,

one frog species is thought to be the most toxic animal in the world. These poisonous frogs warn away predators with brilliant colors of gold or red or blue that say, "Keep off!" (It doesn't help if the predator gets sick *after* he has bitten you in two.) They are commonly known as "poison dart" frogs. Hunters once extracted poisons from frog secretions and used them to tip the points of their blowgun darts. Nowadays, most hunters use shotguns to kill monkeys. But an animal struck by gunshot often dies gripping a tree branch and a hunter must either climb aloft to pry loose his game or wait for hours for it to let go. Not so a monkey or bird struck with a poisoned dart. The animal's muscles relax so that it falls quickly from its perch.

The kinkajou is entirely a creature of the forest canopy. A monkeylike relative of the raccoon weighing five or six pounds, it prowls in the night for fruits and flower nectar. Wrapping its long prehensile tail around a branch, it hangs down to harvest fruit with long-fingered paws.

Yet another canopy resident is the most numerous single species of arboreal mammals in tropical America, the slow-footed three-toed sloth. Food for snakes, eagles, cats, caimans, and native hunters, sloths depend on a survival strategy that puts a premium on keeping still so as not to attract attention.

At night, in the top of a *Cecropia* tree near the water's edge, two sets of small eyes reflect a lantern's light. They belong to a pair of three-toed sloths. The female reclines on a chaise longue of vines. With her neck made extra long by nine vertebrae, she can turn her head to chew on nearby leaves without moving her body. The male sits comfortably in an easy chair formed by the joining of a branch to the trunk. He holds a broad *Cecropia* leaf like a slice of watermelon, munching steadily with small peglike teeth. Alarmed by the light, they turn away slowly and solidify into shapeless lumps.

Except to find better browse, to defecate, and to seek mates, sloths never descend from their treetop haunts. Once thought to eat nothing but leaves of the *Cecropia* tree, a fare shunned by other herbivores, sloths actually enjoy a varied diet, choosing from the foliage and fruits of up to ninety different trees and vines. Sloths also were thought to occupy a single tree throughout their entire thirty-year life span. Not so. A sloth may favor a special food tree, but it uses other trees as well within a radius of about 125 feet.

Researchers have far more questions than answers about the rain forest and its denizens. How has the discovery and description

Poison Dart Frog
Dendrobates pumilio

As its Latin name suggests, it is a "tiny tree-climbing frog," but good defenses help it to be boss frog within water-filled bromeliad battlements. Costa Rican forest people observed that this little creature was carefully avoided by predators, who took warning at its brilliant colors. Hunters learned to extract a deadly poison from the secretions of the frog's skin. When applied to blow-gun dart tips, the poison was a sure killer of monkeys and large birds. The frog combines bright colors and poisonous secretions in a defense mechanism biologists call *aposematic,* or warning, coloration.

following spread

Chirripo National Park
Costa Rica

Pale-mandibled Araçari

Pteroglossus erythropygius

A gregarious fruit-eater, this close cousin of the big-billed toucan makes his home on the Pacific side, or western flank, of the Andes Mountains in South America. Unhappily, its high-altitude habitat is also favored by humans for farms and ranches, and development has all but eliminated the forested areas in which the araçari is endemic. Small populations continue to exist in forest fragments where the flowering and fruiting trees they require are still in evidence. Araçaris forage noisily through the canopy in pairs or small groups, with one bird leading, the others following. Basically vegetarian, they still will rob the nests of other birds.

of 1.4 million species mattered to humankind? If 99 million species remain undescribed, is it worth it to record the identity of yet more creatures that we've never met and haven't missed?

Can we forego the new information and biological wealth that the tropics might share—undiscovered medicines, nourishing foods as yet unknown, assets or knowledge in fields that can scarcely be imagined? Shall we destroy the matrix of green plants vital to clean air and water and a life-sustaining climate? Can we ignore the myriad creatures that contribute to an ecosystem that sustains us? Do we dare to reduce wildlife to the plight of the last surviving blue macaw in the world, living out his lonely life in northeast Brazil?

Local issues, everyday cares, and the demands of living may occupy us. But let's not forget that concern for the wildlife—and wildlife habitats—of tropical America equates with a broader concern for humankind.

Swallow-tailed Cotinga
Phibalura flavirostris

In the ninety species of the cotinga family are some of the rain forest's most spectacularly colored and entertaining birds. As many cotingas are solitary and secretive, living in the topmost branches of the canopy, little is known about some of them. One of these, the swallow-tailed cotinga, is found only in a narrow strip of highland forest in coastal Brazil such as that preserved in the Itatiaia National Park. The swallow-tailed cotinga male, shown here, helps incubate his female's eggs.

Guianan Squirrel
Sciurus aestuans

At home on the forest floor, but more often found in the canopy, Guianan squirrels are widespread and common throughout rain forests at all altitudes, perhaps because they are not hunted. They are the only squirrels in most of their geographic range. Feeding alone in the daytime on nuts, fruit, and tree bark, they are territorial, and will drive away food competitors.

Kinkajou

Potus flavus

Arboreal mammals closely related to the raccoons, kinkajous spend their lives in the forest canopy, feeding at night on fruit. Tolerant of people, kinkajous may be found in gardens and plantations as well as in rain forests, jumping energetically from tree to tree and calling noisily. For rain forest visitors, the kinkajou may be the mammal most likely to be seen, especially at night. Adults are hunted for their meat; juveniles are captured and kept as pets. The name kinkajou is of Indian origin.

Red-and-green Macaw

Ara chloroptera

Among the largest of the parrots, the red-and-green macaw exceeds three feet in length. They range over a widespread territory in both lowland and montane rain forest in search of their preferred food of fruits and nuts. Pairs mate for life, but usually join others in loosely organized flocks of up to thirty or more. Like most other macaws they are noisy, squawking and screeching in flight and during feeding, as well. Their fondness for eating clay as an aid in digestion brings large flocks of red-and-green macaws to riverside embankments where ecotourists gather to watch them gouge out clay to eat.

Blue-and-yellow Macaw

Ara ararauna

Of the eleven species of macaws that brighten the lowland rain forests of the American tropics, none is more colorful than the blue-and-yellow macaw. Favoring habitats near rivers and congregating in flocks of up to thirty, blue-and-yellow macaws are fruit eaters with powerful hooked beaks that they use in climbing about in the upper canopy of trees. Large birds, up to thirty-three inches in length, they can fly long distances in search of food. Mating for life, a macaw pair may build a nest high in a tree, appropriate a woodpecker hole, or dig a cavity into a termite nest. The generic name *Ara* is a Tupi Indian word for "bird."

A lowland forest dweller, this smaller cousin of the big-billed toucan family lives mostly in Brazilian rain forests such as the Itatiaia National Park. Its beak is smaller than those of toucans, but still large enough to allow it to crush the rinds of fruit from *Cecropia* trees and to gobble up insects, lizards, figs, and even the chicks of other birds. The generic name, *Selenidera,* describes the moon-shaped collar at the nape of the neck. The species name, *maculirostris,* explains that there is a spot on the bird's bill.

Spot-billed Toucanet
Selenidera maculirostris

Red-breasted Toucan
Ramphastos dicolorus

If tropical America has a mascot, it is the toucan. With its comically large bill, its bright colors, and its gravelly cry, any of the forty-two species of toucans earns instant recognition and a place in the hearts of residents from Mexico to Argentina. The red-breasted toucan, one of the largest of the genus, reaches a length of nearly two feet. It is also known as the green-billed toucan. The generic name *Ramphastos* explains that the bird "owns a big bill," while the species name, *dicolorus,* indicates that it has variegated colors.

Toco Toucan
Ramphastos toco

Some authorities suggest that the toucan's huge bill may help birds of the same species recognize each other. Others think it may be useful in frightening away predators, as toucans are often exposed in the upper canopy. Although the bill looks large and heavy, it is not. Its sides are thin and lightly constructed. To conceal its signature feature, a toucan has a hinged tail that it can fold up over its head and bill. Toucans are largely fruit eaters, but will eat small animals and birds as well. The species name *toco* is the Guarani Indian word for toucan.

Black-handed Spider Monkey
Ateles geoffroyi

Also known as the Central American spider monkey, this medium-sized monkey is found all the way from western Mexico through Central America down to the west coast of Colombia and Ecuador. A vegetarian competing with the three-toed sloth for leaves, fruits, and flowers, this monkey forages the canopy in small family groups of up to thirty-five members. Long-limbed and slender-bodied, with a long prehensile tail, it is an aerial artist, leaping great distances between tree branches and hanging by its tail to feed. An endangered species, the black-handed spider monkey suffers both from hunting and from loss of the undisturbed forest it requires.

Common Squirrel Monkey
Saimiri sciureus

Little fellows no more than a foot tall and weighing just a couple of pounds, common squirrel monkeys are widely distributed in the lowland rain forests where they range through treetops in groups of anywhere from 20 to 100. Efficient feeders, they search out fruit and tender vegetation, but are also fond of insects. While vocalizing constantly in shrill squeals and yelps, a squirrel monkey troop crashes through trees without concern for noise. Surprisingly, their long tails are not prehensile.

Green Honeycreeper

Chlorophanes spiza

Kin to the colorful tanagers, this five-inch-long nectar sipper lives in the topmost foliage of the evergreen canopy in lowland and lower montane rain forests. It feeds mostly on flower nectaries, but also eats fruit, berries, and insects. The green honeycreeper's generic name, *Chlorophanes,* means "shining green." Its species name, *spiza,* is the Greek word for "finch." Taxonomists retained the name while giving the bird a separate classification.

Plush-crested Jay

Cyanocorax chrysops

Jays all seem to share the same characteristics, being noisy, active, and aggressive, but also unmistakably colorful and distinctive. The plush-crested jay, for example, is more than a foot tall with a black head surmounted with a crest seemingly made of black plush on top of body and wings of several shades of bright blue. Busy feeders, jays will eat almost anything, including the eggs and chicks of other birds, but mostly insects, fruit, nuts, seeds, worms, and lizards. The generic name *Cyanocorax* translates as dark blue, while *chrysops* means "shining like gold" in Greek.

Favoring the broken highlands of montane rain forests, the sulfur-winged parakeet can be found at altitudes as high as 10,000 feet. Growing to a length of about nine inches, it gathers in small flocks of a dozen or so to forage along the edges of open spaces or in the tops of the canopy, often preferring cut-over or second-growth areas. Sulfur-winged parakeets like to get together and preen each other, a grooming behavior known as allopreening. The genus's name *Pyrrhura* calls attention to its reddish tail; the species was described in the nineteenth century by a German explorer named Carl Hoffmann.

Sulfur-winged Parakeet
Pyrrhura hoffmanni

Three-toed Sloth

Bradypus tridactylus

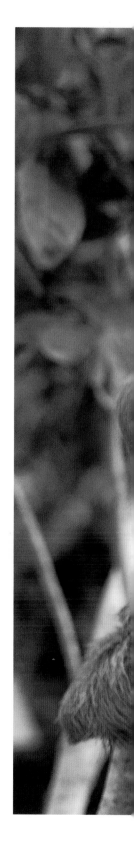

Among the most numerous and widespread of rain forest mammals, sloths possess an effective survival strategy. When a threat is perceived, they freeze into utter immobility and blend so well with the trees in which they feed and live that they seem to disappear. Despite their enemies, which include harpy eagles, large snakes, and crocodiles, sloths do well throughout the rain forest. Their wiry, elongated bodies have so little meat on them that forest people disdain to kill them for food. Virtually helpless on the forest floor, they descend once a week to defecate, at which time they are vulnerable to predation.

Mantled Howler Monkey
Alouatta palliata

More often heard than seen, howler monkeys of several species range throughout Central and South American rain forests where their protracted roars and coughs can be heard for miles. Daytime feeders, groups call to each other at dawn and at dusk. Mantled howler monkeys stand about two feet tall and weigh up to twenty pounds. Sturdy prehensile tails help them move slowly and carefully through the canopy in search of fruit and tender leaves. Although they are able to survive in small forest fragments and are often seen in parks and archaeological sites, mantled howlers are among the most endangered of the howler monkeys due to habitat loss.

Violet-Fronted Brilliant Hummingbird
Heliodoxa leadbeateri

Of the 320 species of New World hummingbirds, most live in tropical America, ranging from the lowest to highest elevations of the rain forest. Any given habitat may harbor as many as fifteen species. The rain forest is well suited to hummingbirds, which depend for survival on the year-round availability of nectar from flowering tropical plants. The tiny birds, in turn, pollinate the flowers to insure survival of the host plants. To a diet of nectar, some hummingbirds add insects. Here, a violet-fronted brilliant sips nectar from a fuchsia blossom in the cloud forest of the Peruvian Andes. In Greek, *Heliodoxa* means "glorious sun."

To an outsized bill, this hummingbird adds an outsized tail, giving it an overall length of six inches. The name of its genus, *Phaethornis*, derives from two Greek words meaning "sun bird." Its species name describes its unique "eyebrows" that indeed give it a supercilious look. Like other hermit hummingbirds, *superciliosus* uses its long bill to sip nectar from deep throated flowers such as those of the *Heliconia*. Females build their nest cups of plant fibers secured to a banana or *Heliconia* leaf.

Long-tailed Hermit Hummingbird
Phaethornis superciliosus

Common Potoo
Nyctibius griseus

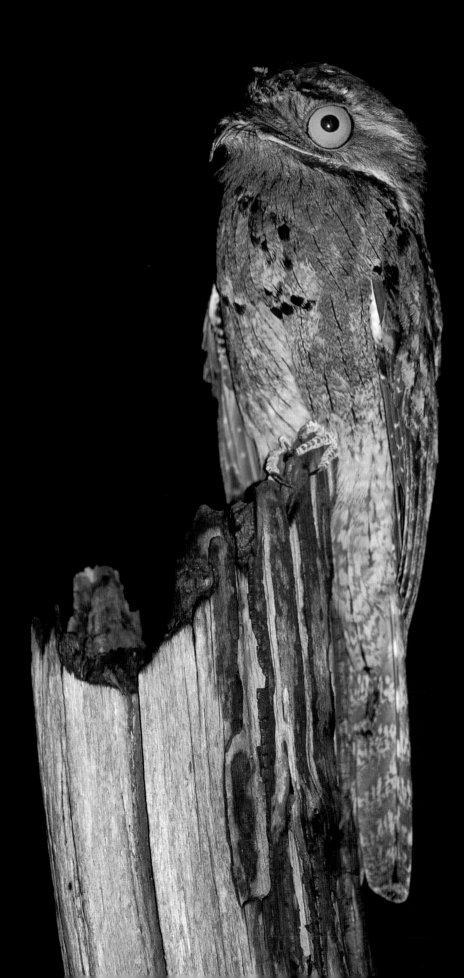

A master of disguise, the potoo conceals itself in plain view by imitating the end of a dead branch and remaining absolutely still throughout the daytime hours. At night, the potoo opens its huge yellow eyes and utters mournful hooting calls. Growing to a length of about fourteen inches, the potoo feeds exclusively on large insects, such as beetles and moths that emerge after dark. Its habitat ranges from the lowlands into the foothills of the montane rain forest, but it is a solitary creature, uniting with a mate only to reproduce.

Great Dusky Swift

Cypseloides senex

Most birds fly, but none has so mastered the air as have the swifts. Small birds—the great dusky swift reaches a length of just seven inches—swifts eat, drink, mate, and possibly even sleep on the wing. They perform phenomenal high-speed acrobatics in pursuit of their insect prey. When they alight to roost or nest, they favor cliff faces near waterfalls or swift streams. As different species of swifts are similar in appearance, it is difficult to tell them apart when they are soaring on high.

Chestnut Woodpecker
Celeus elegans

The scientific name describes the bird appropriately as "elegant woodpecker." Nearly a foot long, it sports a long, powerful bill that enables it to forage for ants in the forest canopy and to hammer open arboreal termite nests for their contents. The chestnut woodpecker seeks out *Cecropia* trees, which harbor ants, and is occasionally spotted in coco plantations and fruit orchards. Uncommon and seldom seen, the chestnut woodpecker inhabits forests from sea level to 2,500 feet.

Red-lored Parrot
Amazona autumnalis

A chunky, short-tailed member of the parrot family, the red-lored parrot takes its name from the frontlet of red feathers between its eyes and the base of its beak, a space called the lore. Growing to around thirteen inches in length, red-lored parrots mate for life, and mates are always seen close to each other, even though pairs gather in large groups to feed and socialize. Preferring lowland rain forest ranging up into foothills, red-lored parrots search for fruits and nuts of palm and other large trees, but also favor mangoes and citrus. The genus name *Amazona* dates back to descriptions by Spanish explorers in the sixteenth century.

Rain Forest Organizations

The following organizations are active in the conservation of the tropical rain forests of Latin America.

Association for Tropical Biology
P. O. Box 1897
Lawrence, KS 66044-8897
Tel: 800-627-0629
Fax: 913-943-1274

Conservation International
2501 M Street NW, Suite 200
Washington, DC 20037
Tel: 800-406-2306
Fax: 202-887-0192

Cultural Survival
96 Mount Auburn Street
Cambridge, MA 02138
Tel: 617-441-5400
Fax: 617-441-5417

Earthwatch
P. O. Box 403
Watertown, MA 02272
Tel: 617-926-8200

Environmental Defense Fund
257 Park Avenue South
New York, NY 10010
Tel: 800-684-3322

Friends of the Earth
1025 Vermont Avenue NW,
3rd Floor
Washington, DC 20005
Tel: 202-783-7400
Fax: 202-784-0444

Fundacion Gaia Amazonas
Carrera 4, # 26B-31, Ofi. 101
Bogota, Colombia
Tel: 57 1 281 4925
Fax: 57 1 281 4945

Instituto del Tercer Mundo
Jackson 1136
Montevideo 11200
Uruguay
Fax: 598 2 401 9222

National Arbor Day Foundation
100 Arbor Avenue
Nebraska City, NE 68410
Tel: 402-474-5655
postmaster@arborday.org

National Wildlife Federation
8925 Leesburg Pike
Vienna, VA 22184
Tel: 703-790-4000

Natural Resources Defense
Council
40 West 20th Street
New York, NY 10011
Tel: 212-727-2700

The Nature Conservancy
4245 North Fairfax Drive
Suite 100
Arlington, VA 22203-1606
Tel: 703-841-5300

Organization for Tropical Studies
P. O. Box DM
Duke Station
Durham, NC 27706
Tel: 919-684-5774

Rainforest Alliance
65 Bleecker Street
New York, NY 10012-2420
Tel: 212-677-1900
Fax: 212-677-2187

Selby Gardens
811 South Shores Boulevard
Sarasota, FL 34236
Tel: 813-366-5730

Smithsonian Tropical Research
Institute
P. O. Box 2072
Panama
Republic of Panama
Tel: 507-227-6022
Fax: 507-232-5978
www.stri.org

Tropical Science Center
P. O. Box 8-3870
San Jose 1000
Costa Rica
Tel: 506-253-3276/3308
Fax: 506-253-4963
cecitrop@sol.racsa.co.cr
www.cct.or.cr/cusin_in.htm

Wildlife Conservation International
Bronx Zoo
185th Street and Southern
Boulevard
Bronx, NY 10460
Tel: 718-220-5090

The Woods Hole Research Center
P. O. Box 296
Woods Hole, MA 02543
Tel: 508-540-9900

World Wildlife Fund US
1250 24th Street NW
Washington, DC 20037
Tel: 202-293-4800

Index

A

Aenea panariste, 89
Agalychnis callidryas, 54
Agouti
   Agouti taczanowskii, 67
   Dasyprocta punctata, 60
Alouatta
   fusca, 92–93
   palliata, 114–115
   pigra, 92
   seniculus, 76–77
Amazona autumnalis, 139
Amazon River, 20–21, 22, 23, 36
Anaconda, 40, 41, 42
Angel Falls, 24, 25
Anodorhynchus hyacinthinus, 114
Anteater, silky, 69, 75, 94–95
Ants
   army, 38, 39
   leaf-cutter, 75, 102
Aotus trivirgatus, 101
Aposematic coloration, 117
Ara
   ararauna, 124
   chloroptera, 124
   macao, 21
Araçari, pale-mandibled, 120
Army ants, 38, 39
Ateles geoffroyi, 128
Atta cephalotes, 102

B

Basiliscus plumifrons, 65
Basilisk, double-crested, 65
Bats, 77, 96, 116
Bear, spectacled, 4, 52–53
Bees, orchid, 79–80
Biodiversity, 20, 26
Birds, 110–111, 114
   acorn woodpecker, 82
   blue-and-yellow macaw, 124
   broad-billed motmot, 64
   capped heron, 64
   chestnut woodpecker, 139
   cock-of-the-rock, 78–79
   common potoo, 137
   crimson-crested woodpecker, 82
   great dusky swift, 138
   green-billed toucan, 126
   green honeycreeper, 130
   guira cuckoo, 97

   hoatzin, 104
   hyacinth macaw, 114
   large-billed tern, 26–27
   long-tailed hermit hummingbird, 136
   ocellated turkey, 46
   owls, 78
   pale-mandibled araçari, 120
   plush-crested jay, 130
   quetzal, 110–111
   red-and-green macaw, 124
   red-breasted toucan, 126
   red-rumped cacique, 26, 27
   royal flycatcher, 28
   rufous-tailed jacamar, 105
   scarlet macaw, 21
   screaming piha, 110
   spot-billed toucanet, 126
   sulfur-winged parakeet, 131
   toco toucan, 127
   violet-fronted brilliant hummingbird, 136
   yellow-bellied elaenia, 83
Botflies, 26
Brachycephalus ephippium, 54–55
Brachyteles arachnoides, 100
Bradypus tridactylus, 132–133
Brazil trees, 38
Brockets, 47
Bromeliads, 71
Bush dog, 39, 61
Butterflies, 43, 74–75
   common morpho, 103
   leaf-mimic, 75, 88, 89
   leaf miner, 103
   sulfur, 43

C

Cacicus haemorrhous, 26, 27
Cacique, red-rumped, 26, 27
Caiman *(Caiman crocodilus),* 33, 42–43, 66–67
Callicebus moloch, 98–99
Callithrix jacchus, 80
Camouflage, 88
Campephilus melanoleucos, 82
Canaima Lagoon, 30–31
Canaima National Park, 30, 71
Capuchins, 70–71, 78, 106–107
Capybara, 40
Cayambe-Coca Reserve, 81
Cebus
   capucinus, 106–107
   olivaceus, 70–71
Celeus elegans, 139
Centrolenella spp., 103
Chirripo National Park, 118–119
Chlorophanes spiza, 130
Choerododis strumaria, 88
Coati, 39, 86
Cock-of-the-rock, 69, 78–79

Cockle-shell orchid, 70
Coendou prehensilis, 60
Coloration
   aposematic, 117
   cryptic, 88
Colubridae spp., 75
Cotinga, swallow-tailed, 121
Crocodiles. *See* Caiman
Crotalus durissus, 56–57
Crypsis, 88
Cuckoo, guira, 97
Cyanocorax chrysops, 130
Cyclopes didactylus, 94–95
Cypseloides senex, 138

D

Deer, red brocket, 47
Deforestation, 77, 107, 114, 120, 128
Dendrobates pumilio, 116, 117
Dog, bush, 39, 61

E

Eciton burchelli, 38, 39
Ectophylla alba, 96
Eira barbara, 57
Elaenia, yellow-bellied, 83
Elaenia flavogaster, 83
Electron platyrhynchum, 64
El Yunque, 112–113
Epiphytic plants, 71, 74
Eunectes notaeus, 41

F

Fer-de-lance, 38
Flycatchers, 28, 111
Frogs, 46, 54, 116
   glass, 103
   gold, 54–55
   leaf, 68, 87
   poison dart, 109, 116, 117
   red-eyed tree, 32, 46, 54
   red-webbed tree, 1

G

Galbula ruficauda, 105
Grasshoppers
   lichen-mimic, 88, 91
   moss-mimic, 11, 88, 90
   stick-mimic, 88, 90
Guianan Shield, 24
Guira guira, 97

H

Habitat loss, 77, 107, 114, 120, 128
Heliodoxa leadbeateri, 136
Heron, capped, 64
Herpailurus yaguarondi, 84–85
Hoatzin, 104
Honeycreeper, green, 130

Howler monkeys, 76–78, 92–93, 109, 114–115
Hummingbirds, 109, 110–111, 136
Hydrochaeris hydrochaeris, 40

I

Iguaçú Falls National Park, 43
Indigenous peoples, 23
Itatiaia National Park, 121, 126

J

Jacamar, rufous-tailed, 105
Jaguar, 43, 46, 58–59,
    jaguar tracks, 19, 144
Jaguarundi, 69, 75, 84–85

K

Katydid, leaf-mimic, 88, 89
Keystone species, 79
Kinkajou, 116, 117, 123

L

Leaf miner, 69, 103
Leopardus
    pardalis, 58–59
    wiedii, 28–29

M

Macaws, 111, 114
    blue-and-yellow, 124
    hyacinth, 114
    red-and-green, 108, 124
    scarlet, 19, 21
Manaus, 21
Mangroves, 38
Manu Wildlife Refuge, 40
Margay, 28–29, 75, 116
Marmosets, 78, 80
Mazama americana, 47
Melanerpes formicivorous, 82
Meleagris ocellata, 46
Monkeys, 74, 77–78
    brown titi, 8, 98–99
    capuchin, 70–71, 78, 106–107
    howler, 76–78, 92–93, 109, 114–115
    marmoset, 78, 80
    night, 101
    owl, 101
    spider, 19, 77, 100, 128
    squirrel, 77, 129
    tamarin, 78
Monteverde cloud forest, 72–73
Morpho peleides, 103
Motmot, broad-billed, 64
Muriqui, 77, 100

N

Napo River, 44–45
Nasua narica, 86
Neotropics, 23

Night monkey, 101
Nyctibius griseus, 137

O

Ocelot, 48–49
Oncilla, 75
Onychorhynchus coronatus, 28
Opisthocomus hoazin, 104
Opossums, 75
Orchids, 70, 71, 79–80
Orinoco River, 23
Otter, giant river, 11, 40, 62–63
Owl monkey, 101
Owls, 78

P

Pacas, 60, 61, 67
Paddle trees, 38
Palm trees, 38
Panthera onca, 48–49
Pará, 21
Parakeet, sulfur-winged, 131
Parrots, 108, 111, 114, 139
Passionflower, 27
Peccary, collared, 51
Phaethornis superciliosus, 136
Phaetusa simplex, 26–27
Pharomachrus mocinno, 110–111
Phibalura flavirostris, 121
Phoebis sp., 43
Phyllomedusa vaillanti, 87
Piha, screaming, 110
Pilherodius pileatus, 64
Podocnemis unifilis, 42
Porcupines, 60, 77
Potoo, common, 137
Potus flavus, 123
Praying mantis, leaf-mimic, 88
Pteroglossus erythropygius, 120
Pteronura brasiliensis, 62–63
Pyrrhura hoffmanni, 131

Q

Quetzal, resplendent, 110–111

R

Rain forests
    benefits of, 24, 26
    biodiversity of, 20, 26
    cleared for agriculture, 23
    layers of, 24
    rainfall in, 20
    types of, 23–24
Ramphastos
    dicolorus, 126
    toco, 127
Rattlesnake, Yucatan neotropical, 56–57
Reed stem orchid, 32
Rio Napo, 36–37

Rio Negro, 21
Rio Solimoes, 21
River of the Calabash Trees, 36
Rupicola peruviana, 78

S

Saimiri sciureus, 129
Sciurus aestuans, 122
Selenidera maculirostris, 126
Sloth, three-toed, 117, 132–133
Snakes, 74–75
    anaconda, 40, 41, 42
    colubrid, 75
    fer-de-lance, 38
    Yucatan neotropical rattlesnake, 56–57
Speothus venaticus, 61
Spider monkeys, 77, 100, 128
Spotted orchid, 71
Squirrel, Guianan, 122
Squirrel monkeys, 77, 129
Swift, great dusky, 138

T

Tamarin monkeys, 78
Tapir, Brazilian, 50
Tapirus terrestris, 50
Tayassu tajacu, 51
Tayra, 57
Tepuis, 24
Tern, large-billed, 26–27
Tettigoniidae spp., 90, 91
Torrid Zone, 20, 23
Toucanet, spot-billed, 126
Toucans, 110
    green-billed, 126
    red-breasted, 11, 126
    toco, 127
Trees, 38, 71, 74, 79
Tremarctos ornatus, 4, 52–53
Trogons, 110–111
Turkey, ocellated, 46
Turtle, yellow-spotted Amazon River, 42
Typophyllum mortuifolium, 89

U

Uroderma bilobatum, 96
Utropidacris cristata, 90

W

Woodpeckers, 78
    acorn, 82
    chestnut, 18, 139
    crimson-crested, 82